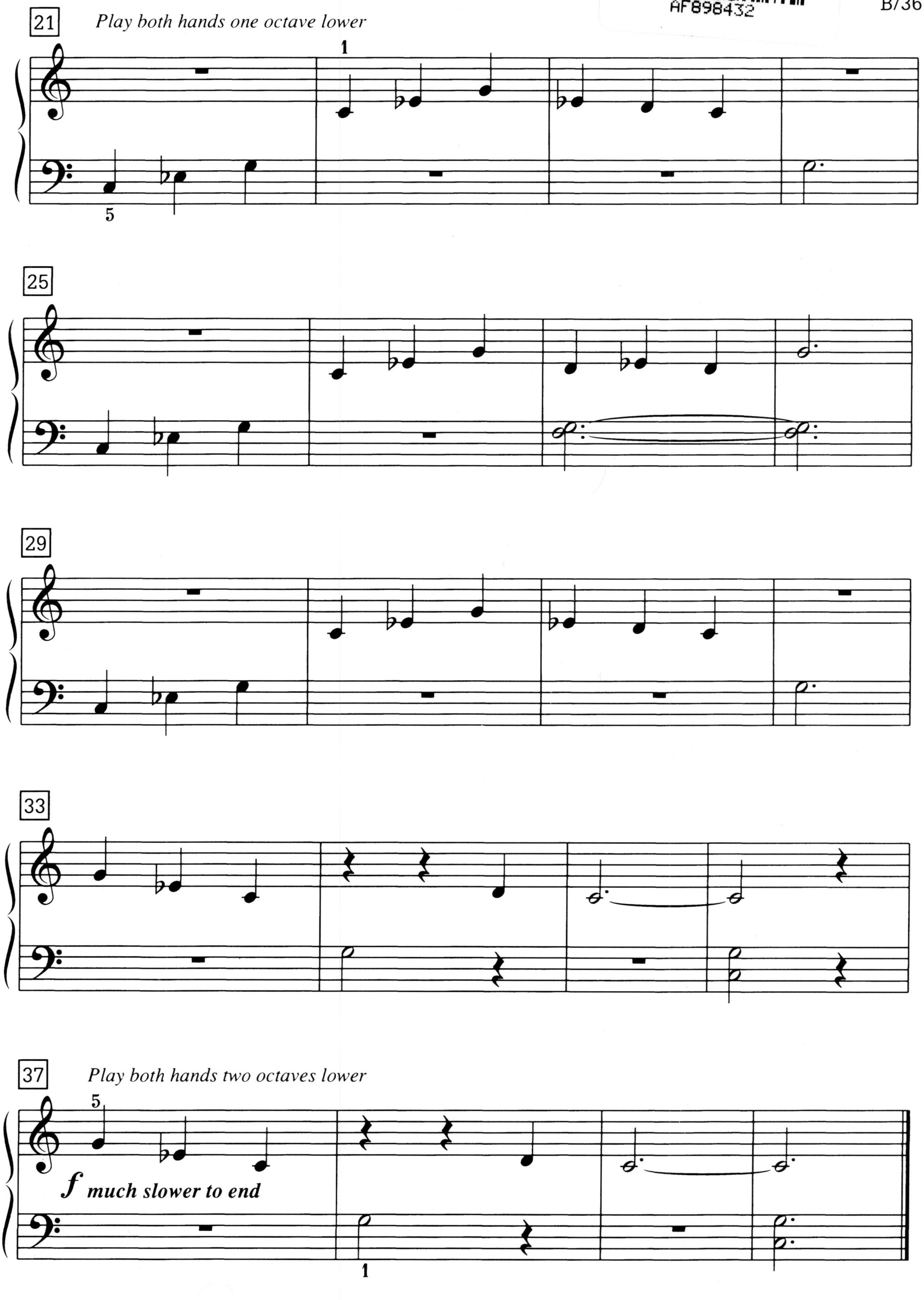
21
Play both hands one octave lower
25
29
33
37
Play both hands two octaves lower
f much slower to end

Alfred's Basic Piano Library

Willard A. Palmer • Morton Manus • Amanda Vick Lethco

A PIANO COURSE FOR BEGINNERS OF ALL AGES

Alfred's Basic Piano Library offers nine perfectly graded beginning series which are designed to prepare students of all ages for a successful musical learning experience. With the exception of **Alfred's Basic Adult Piano Course,** which is complete in itself, all of the beginning series are interchangeable at several levels (see arrows below), and lead into the main **Alfred's Basic** course, which is complete through Level 6 (seven levels all together). This course, then, is the most flexible of any method in allowing the teacher to personally design a specific curriculum according to the age and needs of each individual student. On completion, the student is ready to begin playing the great piano masterworks.

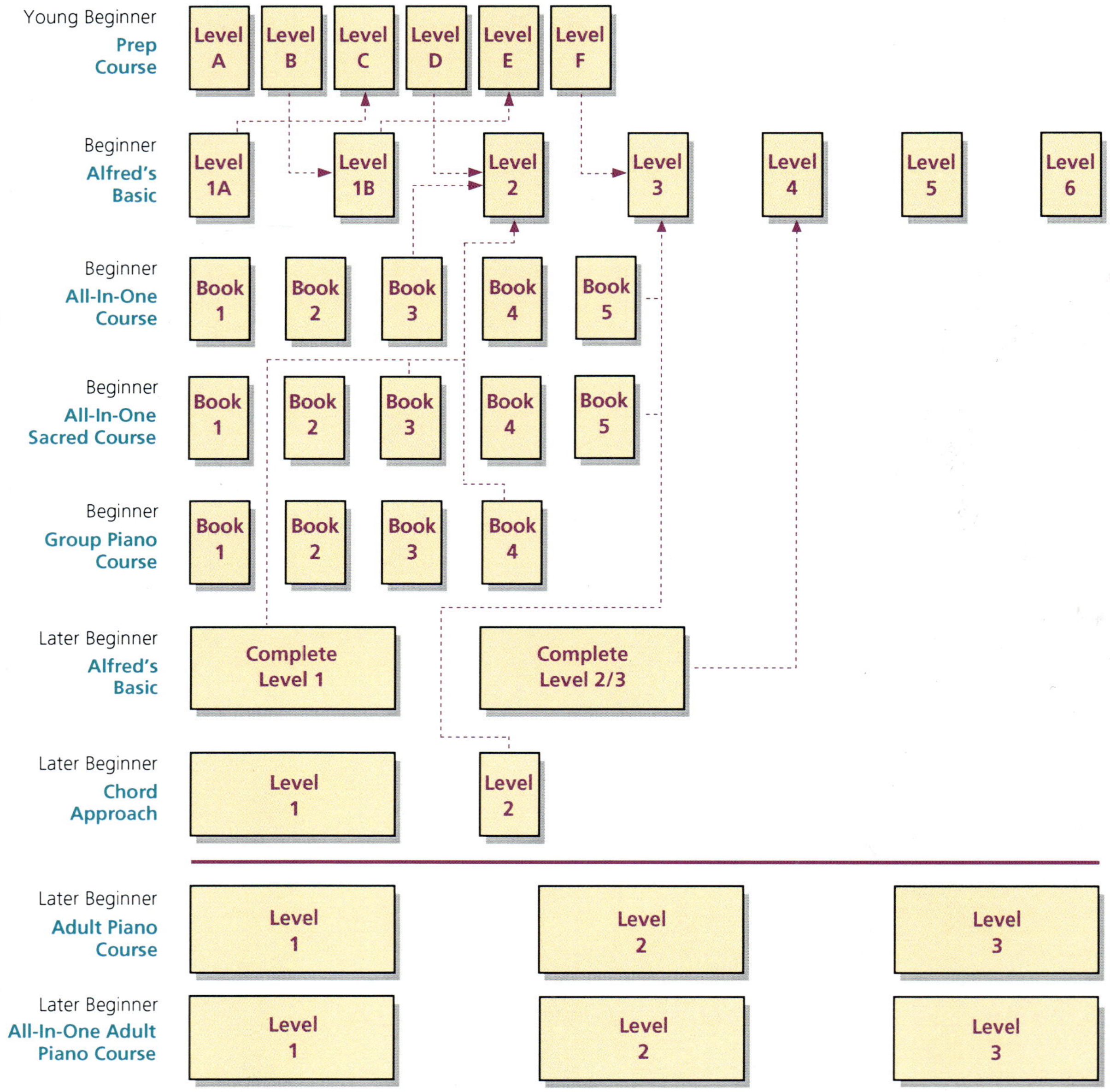

alfred.c

ISBN-10: 0-7390-1336-X
ISBN-13: 978-0-7390-1336-6

9 780739 013366

9780739013366

ISBN 0-7390-1336-X

Alfred's Basic Piano Library Prep Course

Prep Course Level B

Gold Doubloons

Martha Mier

Alfred

Gold Doubloons

Boldly

Martha Mier